Sublingual

poems by

Joan Naviyuk Kane

Finishing Line Press
Georgetown, Kentucky

Sublingual

ACKNOWLEDGMENTS

Grateful acknowledgement is made to the editors of the following publications, in which versions of these poems have appeared or are forthcoming:

Academy of American Poets Poem-A-Day series ("Gray Eraser")
Alaska Quarterly Review ("Starvation Episode")
Arkansas International ("A Few Lines with Monique Sanchez," "A Few Lines with Sherman Alexie," and "A Few Lines with Abigail Chabitnoy")
Colorado Review ("White Alice Changes Hands")
FLAG + VOID ("Wellhead")
the *Guardian* ("Visitors")
Kin ("Polynya")
Orion ("To List")
the Peabody Essex Museum ("A Few Lines with Terese Maillhot" and "A Few Lines with Bill Wetzel")
Pinwheel ("A Few Lines with Sherwin Bitsui," "A Few Lines with Darlene Naponse," and "Milk Black Carbon,")
Wasafiri ("Dark Passage," and "Darker Passage")
Yellow Medicine Review ("A Few Lines with…")

Publisher: Leah Maines
Editor: Christen Kincaid
Cover Art: Joan Kane, digital art based on photograph copyright Chris Lott
Author Photo: Joan Naviyuk Kane
Cover Design: Leah Huete

Printed in the USA on acid-free paper.
Order online: www.finishinglinepress.com
also available on amazon.com

Author inquiries and mail orders:
Finishing Line Press
P. O. Box 1626
Georgetown, Kentucky 40324
U. S. A.

Table of Contents

DARK TRAFFIC

"Yes, melting changes / the whole picture"
—James Merrill

& the snows buffer the sound of a voice set forth.

> *I thought you lost already, that you had gone*
> *to neglect the late migration*

Before it ceases, the ice collapses easily.
There is no day without a symptom.

Consolation may turn out to be a guttural
practice, after all, the small gesture

of sound lodged deep before it glides
without warning downward.

There is nothing but the wind, a howl
and dive where water is thrown

over water and sown into it.
A howl and dive of wind, water

> *I found flown*

over water where once we found ice,
where the snow once stuttered the sound

of that shouter, shouting, for this listener
holding her head in her hands, the head

in its fine blank way an original.

WELLHEAD

Along-strike, the land is lined with diesel drums corroding over
the corridors of disorder, which is to say—like in an easy rhyme,
though I expect to gain the ground I scan out from here, how?
The depressions deepen through each successive thaw, boring

as usual in the confused, and at times, vehement light. Mother—
I know what it means to exemplify the worst surfeit of a wasted
education, maybe: life. Oil oozes from the abandoned pit
and pock drilled by drone—toolpusher, roustabout, motorman,

whatever—his axe and lone glove thrown under the flawed
cement plug he once poured in weather too cold for any of it.
More than one well shack swells with methane, profane lumber
juts and jags. It remains. I don't think they made a map so much

as a plan to send their pennies down a tight hole. Kill the well
to stop the spill, they say. Contain, bury, comply, and walk away.

MILK BLACK CARBON

Observe the coal dust over boats in the harbor,
the snow load on the glacier. Take in the woman
who pursues a myth to counter another myth.
What dazes, scatters and filters: each respiration
blurs an image. The coal tipple tilts in its new skin.
Meadows blonde. From open shelves, honey jars
tumble to split and spill in the gasp of a temblor.
The thick odor of a nearby smoke will signal the end
of something, not summer. The fire veins as sap does,
translating stands of beetle-killed spruce to crackle
and torch. She cannot hurt too much, too long—
take in the woman you have not become. And
then, take a little breath and hold your breathing.
Breathe, don't move, and hold your breath again.

WHITE ALICE

I

sassaq
sassaq sassaq
sassaq sassaq sassaq
sassaq sassaq sassaq sassaq
sassaq sassaq sassaq
sassaq sassaq
sassaq

II

> *clack the wheels on the wall*
> *as they click the rock of ore*
>
> *for distant brawls bells clang & roll,*
> *& strike within her sawdust clocks*

GRAY ERASER

There is no one to scold,
even when the heavens deem

the most abject of failures
receptive to correction.

Likewise, in cackleless sleep,
the magpies remain tucked away.

A mother can no longer dismiss
her child as a spectacular waste

of an education. Even the wind
stills its sighs in the dry and bare

branches of the nearby white
spruce damaged by Lirula blight.

Meanwhile, a pearl-green fox
retracts its untrussed tail

through an eastward sky
thick with unfamiliar stars.

If I wake missing the cold,
fresh sound of new snow,

I may still miss the kinds of places
that scar me and complete

my sorrow. Late at night,
the birches must let their leaves

pitch and imbricate the floor
of what is left of the woods

near what is left of me.

CUTTING THE RIVER

"These Eskimos might be much more than they seem."
—David Foster Wallace

I woke up like this: on the shore
of a snow-beaten sea
during the dark part of a day
that will darken, like the others,
into the dark winter.

When the tragic figure
thinks of death, he
thinks of me. In this way
I become, at last, another
bright departure.

Haltlose and yet high-fed,
witness the mountain
I make of his grass widow
before her middle,
too, is worn away

with reckless weather.

A FEW LINES WITH TERESE MAILHOT

She loses her belief in nothing
and dreams beyond the mundane.

The sky in its entirety speckles
with weather into the self that opens

to another self, in the way a nipple
gives rise to a reciprocal mountain:

distant figures of some other's land.
The hue of the sky charges neither minor

nor major. A mother a kind of puncture.
A path narrow and speechless

and not made smaller by vastness
fair and fast. All the disloyalties

in the silt-laden stream puddle underfoot
into sororal darkness. How her heart

beat the summer day clear and bright,
and brought her closer to her son.

How the belt that binds her belly
will fix him to her back, breathed

and slung to sleep, to conceive
of his own son yet to come,

gesturing her, to her, visible
to us, even at the edge

of the green wall of memory
and the loud blood of lost days.

DARK PASSAGE

"...whatever it can seize floating on the surface..."
—Anna Komnene

The fatherless child is taught to swim by his abandoned mother—
mouths on the mainland erase them as she casts him down
into the fishlessness of the black lake pooled from ice-melt

on ice on the isle on which they live, together, distant
from those who banished them. His small palms grasp
a sealskin scraper, once wood. The water buoys his body.

Between rainfall and unnamed waves, he shall rehearse
the flooded world she forgets and loses then fails
to remember when they help two hunters come to pass

upon their land, alive with the drift meat of the rare carcass—
men sent to kill. The boy has grown to swim at sea,
yet it occurs to me not to demonstrate a story

I am not to tell—for spit in the ocean, there is no end but wind.

QUONDAM HYSTERESIS

is it the clavicle absent
the sun a hung thing

     the horse hooves they cannot find
          purchase on ice

a hinge its red unhealing sore
just over the earth's arc

and then again gone

a confusion of blood done
     again into blood

carved light in the vise grip
walrus tusk scrap and then gone

again on Front St a cop makes an arrest
mindless to the widening dilation

the compact man gone limp
his arms complication-laden

     she with forgotten labors foregoes
     the grieved grave
          the ward a cheap
     fluorescence the daughter they collapse

old house disused rock peaks
sea-roused   alike we shall bury

be buried but to poise a seal
oil globule   upon caribou-marrow broth

and postpone from blow to moment
that which set me down long ago

A FEW LINES WITH ABIGAIL CHABITNOY

Maybe we could stand in the sun until
someone tells us how bad things will get

This too is about where the heart isn't   See a woman
trudged near, cradling bones

not loss or lack but something as real as
my slate knife sharpened   To incise

the caribou organs I spurn in assembly
but bring to my mother as my children

rustle the leaves of our drowned taiga   Englut men
with ambition   recall the ocean   *sentinel perdu*

DARKER PASSAGE

It has been bound with rope
& the weapons of a child

   this land with its laws
   serving as wire & root

to bind us together Sinew snare the unseen growth
of the green tree many rivers south whose stump now shoals into use

The wire itself works its way through layer upon layer
of land submerged of ice of ash though lakes would
be the eyes of the earth A phreatomagmatic blue sprawl the Devil

Mountain maar The Imuruk Basin drains through inland veins
scrawling tributaries in familiar names The giant granite tors at
Serpentine (Iyat, the cooking pot) sentineled in unscoured stone
towering endlessly into the flickering sky

    Auksruaq

   like the blood that seeps across America in such hot & dim
& strenuous times where one still cannot be serene **Red phalarope:
might we follow, leaving the meadow wet with tears?** From nest to
fledge & then to
move again right out to sea circling
   pent
vortices to upwell food Let us lose our grief
in great rafts as we translate the renamed straits

Our limb
Our burnt and broken

                        At last make noise of a truth
together. At length let us return to furrow
                                                furrows
where we made portage with our boats

                        Let us keep

the line taut   we could not **cede** the land with his hands
at our throat   his face betraying a dream   a possession

He lost but
                a hound   a horse and a dove in his seizure of we bereavers
   bereft   reaved of and in it

A FEW LINES WITH SHERMAN ALEXIE

How many Eskimo words are there for *white people?*

    A region of the moon in a snow-blind noon
    Bleached seal skin & wave-smoothed stone

Mouth thronged with *schs* and *ors & knees*
Ears, somewhere, adorned & unable to discern

    is it worry   *is it question*

STARVATION EPISODE

Rifle tobacco tea and cloth
deliver us from this time
when foxes come no longer:

we are vexed with troubles
of love and coalition,
a glut, and what to sustain us?

A FEW LINES WITH MONIQUE SANCHEZ

Of course, I have a question more pressing but—
did the thyme survive the first deep freeze and snow?
how sirens pierce the air thick over the hills,

how pleasurably I defer doing, how stuck—

I quadruple my entendre of shots across the bow
during the most recent epiphanic visitation
of Barbara Johnson incarnate, who, like you,
will continue to remind me to heed my proximity

to myself at all times. *No gold here,* I heard.
It could have been *Z. atricapilla*, its summer thrum
dimmed by gloom and calm that escapes me now

in October, the precursor to the dark winter
before the bright one that stirs when the light
blitzes back at the turn of the year. If only impaired

while permitted to be so all morning—if only I had not
tried to train various vines to climb and flower. If only
I'd burnt the birch branches I gathered, if only some last light

thronged the trees and interpreted green as green though—
green thought, though green, thyme-leaved, thyme-fed.

TO LIST

The boat rocks back and forth over the waters as they rise
while the land where women bleed all the time
recedes from sight. Its trouble of moss and stubble

throngs with pests: the ilk of men who malign
their mothers. And then corrupts into a motherless
tract where children never sleep, though its leaves

grow large, we do not know why. They increase
and do not grow back. The grown leave
and do not go back, the gone grow

and do not go back.

A FEW LINES WITH SHERWIN BITSUI

"He was completely and openly a mess. Meanwhile the rest of us go on trying to fool each other."
—Denis Johnson

The drunk voice of reason hypodescends to the elephant
in the room. Meanwhile, on the drive from Elephant Rock
to Elephant Point there was something about not passing
or passing: it made me more awkward than usual, more
or less visible, shaken and anxious, depressed and aimless
in the way that a bad hangover foregrounds my Eskimo

emptiness. A bad hangover and a bad book idea birdlessly
compound the need to perform to expectations. I think I can
escape the false sense of context surfacing from the stanzas
I happen to make, day after day, all the way back to god-thick
shrines, back before the spilled Guggenwhine, which, after all
serves as a general reminder: squalor, as we know, can work.

Stirring just now from a restorative grotto of pill-and-booze-
induced unconsciousness there list but a few people I loathe
and a smattering whose work I admire, actually. It's a small
community that discusses and lives amid this stuff all the time.
That wine from the last stanza was good, and not just because
it was wine. Thank you for inviting me to bring it over to this

one. And per contra, the large general audience has little or no
predicate in the issues. *Pibloktoq.* In their human analogy,
this poem, unlike the last one, is already over, over and over.

DARKER TRAFFIC

Changed by rain and become slush
       the end of the open lead
       the tongue's quick
       the quick list
       the quick mouth
       the mouth of a bird
       the bird who bears
       the beak no longer

& caught in the maw of a melt-hole
& merged as wolf

               not broke through snow
               not a blow of the fist

arroba the mercy of the wind...

Our blizzard drifts
and brash ice

cracks

and shelf ice
lifts aloft, recurs
to catch the rust thrust

of a propeller from the outboard
motor. Here we stop. Hear the seals
breathe. Near the maternal den the din

visible like frost-smoke beneath a water
sky. Mind a windbreak wall and listen for the wind-
driven tide: a dark line along the shore we cross and seep.

VISITORS

Every door stands an open door:
our human settlements all temporary.

We share together the incidental shore
and teach the young to tend the lamp's wick,

weary of anyone small enough to bar the exit.

WHITE ALICE CHANGES HANDS

III

Are you yet in a green, green tree—
or is it dry and bled of sap,
cut and black and burnt for fuel?

The anvil clangs, our men are rung.

Will the mountain buck her name
when she obliterates the light?

White Alice, must we go to school?
White Alice, where is God's gold wrist?

I'll rive a river where none exists.

Dark waves work me loose from the net,
insist I drown and drift ashore—White

Alice, will she tell me more?
Would her shields bedarken me?

Will her men have kneeled our men low?

Her men seek lands they should not
see and hold furs that they could not
claim, while she tests our fear and shame—

Could we yet make tumble-down the edges
of her dulling town with its blur

of false-front buildings? The north wind
west and wet besets. This place gets real
rough real fast. White Alice, can I use

your name?

A FEW LINES WITH...

Cedar Sigo, sit down.

I will neither wave a white flag nor settle out of court.
May a blizzard glitter in my bones

until your sea glass is ground to sand.

*

Whilom both the beer
and the bottle done rut

into the cowpath beneath the aerostat tethered long before I was
betrayed, 'twas not long before I knew it so.

*

Although the schism
                    between something thought
                    and something known
                    proffers a vastness habitual
                    and continuous, you see, you must—

pause your perusal of the merch tent at the inquisition.
When, not where, will it all end? In the valley

of a bromidic story, expect me to take an elbow
to the temple. Sistermine, I'll send a placard.

Give it to her.

                    She can use it, too.

A FEW LINES WITH BILL WETZEL

Our hero does cross on his way down to hell his own heart.
Past the bones she bore within: those brittle lines
should not have been. After all, the self's in danger
of transport elsewhere—like pollen, ash, or powder

in a coil of the wind. The mistress of a wealthy man
unwraps to a series of facts, attunement to a world
ringing with broken bells. The mistress of an artist,
orchestrating her vulnerabilities, would bring her

daughter, dressed in local costume, suffering vanity
to such an end. A woman made bereft of both options
holds the smoke that sleeplessly jags on her own __truths.
She collects anything for her new museum. To barter
for beads and ribbons, to have been brought all the way down

like a girl I used to know: she burns what she needs and lets me go.

POLYNYA

It is disproven to me in a dream, the mountain
as weight fixed in place. The lapse of a seal-as-such

lists, then slips from the deep saline of a greater current.
A figure keens on land: no different kind of mammal.

One should pull fish from the hole we conspire together.
Once a girl south-hearted, I grew familiar with the pistons

of her disinterest: bone on bone in a cold, cold bed.

A FEW LINES WITH DARLENE NAPONSE

Stress puking differs from party puking & stress drinking's nothing
like partying. The simile contradicts, which is to say:
Marfa's ornamental trees merely flap in the wind.

I mean adverbially but at least I inflect it with purpose.
How many rules of the brute's brutish language
can I break in one poem? Also, who cares

for prepositions or conjunctions exclusive
of their primitive streaks? No matter I propose
to mount *de novo* as master, a mother,

or remnant. Let them rehearse apology
as in their customs. I stare dust stirred
into my blood. Such paroxysms demolish

the swallow's nest & so, when told to set
out I get on as usual, never not able to note
the corners, the fences, the four dark figures

distant before me for miles before receding,
before I was spooked, truly. The men, all men,
refuse to wave. Their bare hands seem to pray:

invisibility becomes a metaphor. I repeat
our lung gusts. The self, if, as it manages

to survive the cups knocked at once
across the floor, gulps together
on the abandoned page.

WHITE ALICE CHANGES

4

Was there once a live, green tree?
White Alice, will you look at me?

White Alice, why would you come back?

Joan **Naviyuk Kane** is Inupiaq with family from King Island (Ugiuvak) and Mary's Igloo, Alaska. She was raised in and attended public school in Anchorage, where she currently raises her sons as a single mother. Kane graduated with honors from Harvard College, where she was a Harvard National Scholar, and Columbia University's School of the Arts, where she was the recipient of a graduate Writing Fellowship. Her books include *The Cormorant Hunter's Wife* (2009), *Hyperboreal* (2013), *The Straits* (2015), *Milk Black Carbon* (2017), and *A Few Lines in the Manifest* (2018) and *Another Bright Departure* (forthcoming 2019).

She has received the John Haines Award (2004), Rasmuson Foundation Individual Awards (2007, 2016), the Whiting Writer's Award (2009), the Connie Boochever Fellowship from the Alaska Arts and Cultures Foundation (2009), a National Native Creative Development Program Award from the Longhouse Education and Cultural Center (2009), the Anchorage Museum Theatre Script Contest (2009), and was a finalist for the 2009 Poetry Foundation's Ruth Lilly Fellowship. Kane received the 2013 Native Arts and Cultures Foundation National Artist Fellowship, the 2013 United States Artists Foundation Creative Vision Award, the 2013 Rasmuson Foundation Artist Fellowship, the 2014 Alaska Literary Award, and the 2016 Aninstantia Foundation Fellowship. In 2014, she was indigenous writer-in-residence at the School For Advanced Research, was Tuttle Creative Residency Fellow at Haverford College and a Fellow at the Hermitage Artist Retreat in 2016, and, in 2017, was a Lannan Foundation Residency Fellow and a judge for the awards of the Griffin Poetry Prize. She is a 2018 Guggenheim Fellow in Poetry.

Her poems have been anthologized widely, including *Best American Poetry, Hick Poetics, Read America(s), Syncretism & Survival: A Forum on Poetics, Monticello in Mind*, and elsewhere, and new poems have recently appeared or are forthcoming in *Pinwheel, Arkansas International*, and *Boston Review*. Her essays have recently appeared or are forthcoming in *Sustenance: Writers from BC and Beyond on the Subject of Food, The Poem's Country: Place & Poetic Practice*, and *21|19: Readings in Proximity*, and *Exquisite Vessel: Shapes of Native Nonfiction*. She has taught in the low-residency MFA program in writing at the Institute of American Indian Arts in Santa Fe, New Mexico, since January 2014.